Trump vs. Hillary

Uncovering the Truth

Wolf Cooper

CONTENTS

INTRODUCTION

Nothing in the history of the United States has so deeply and clearly divided the nation since the Civil War over a hundred years ago. On November 8th, 2016, Donald Trump was named the United States President-Elect after one of the most vicious, unprecedented elections in history. Even now, months into Trump's administrations, questions are being asked of both sides: how did this happen? What was really going on? Allegations of fraud, of hacks, FBI interference. What's real and what's the truth when both sides of our political spectrum are flinging accusations at each other?

The first fact is this: Hillary Clinton won the popular vote by nearly 2.9 million votes, earning 48.2% of the vote, making her the most voted for losing candidate in history (CNN, 2016). The second fact is that absolutely no evidence of wrongdoing has been found on Hillary Clinton's part, despite many probes into thousands of her emails (LA Times, 2017). The third fact as that Trump has banned news outlets he does not like from attending and reporting on briefings at the White House, including the BBC, CNN, and The Guardian—all known democratic leaning outlets— (The Guardian, 2017). The fourth fact is that Trump has fired the FBI director only after he began a probe into Trump's relations with Russia and the possibility of hacks and voter fraud perpetrated by an alliance between Trump and Russia (MSNBC, 2017). The fifth fact is that during a briefing about the firing of Comey, Trump forbid United States press but allowed in Russia press (New York Times, 2017).

Do these things worry you? They probably should, no matter how one voted, it's clear something very unconstitutional is lurking in the shadows. But for even those who lived through this strange period of American politics aren't entirely sure what's going on, what can be trusted, and what these news rules seem to be.

The fact is, this election featured two of the most unpopular candidates in history, with less than 50% of the country favoring either one of them going into the election. To top that off, this was also an election that was heavily influenced by the ideas and votes of third party voters and young voters. But there were other, less savory influences as well. The belief that Russia had made a puppet out of Trump and mockery of everything else by hacking into our voting system, was something that greatly worried the American people, politicians, and United States investigative branches.

It's one for the record books, and not necessarily in a good way, either. The Electoral College has never come under more fire before for an upset. While several times in the past candidates have won the popular vote but lost the election, never had it been so high profile and by such a wide margin (2.9 million votes for Hillary over Donald Trump). The Electoral College, recently called an archaic system in the wake of all of this, was set up as a way to ensure the people don't succumb to the populist vote and/or elect a dictator. It's the shadow of democracy in the form of the people voting for someone who is going to vote on their behalf. States have different levels of electors to help balance the situation out. In short, it's not the person who gets the most votes but the person who gets the most states who wins the election. And with Trump's popularity in the Midwest, he easily claimed the Electoral College.

But the question should be, where did that mass popularity in the middle of the country come from? The disgruntled "silent majority" that elected Trump president did so because it felt ostracized by the current, progressive administration.

So, how did it happen? How does the country with more personal freedoms than any other country in the world end up so completely distrusting their election system and the players therein and, ultimately, elect what many believe to be the most unqualified candidate in history? This book may not give the most definitive answers, but it will give you facts that can help point our thoughts in the right direction.

THANK YOU FOR BUYING THIS PINNACLE PUBLISHERS BOOK!

Join our mailing list and get updates on new releases, deals, bonus content and other great books from Pinnacle Publishers. We also give away a new eBook every week completely free!

Scan the Above QR Code to Sign Up

Or visit us online to sign up at
www.pinnaclepublish.com/newsletter

CHAPTER 1: THE HISTORY OF THE CLINTON DYNASTY

In a time beyond precedence, Hillary Clinton fits right in. She was the First Lady to husband Governor Bill Clinton and, later, First Lady of the United States when he became the 42nd president. However, she entered politics in her own right when she became the senator for New York, serving from 2001 to 2009 and later was appointed the 67th Secretary of the United States from 2009 to 2013. She ran for president twice and was considered the favorite contender to become the first female president in history.

But it didn't happen. Today Hillary Clinton is a private citizen, offering interviews to press and talks with public audiences, serving as a commentator and worried voter while continuing to watch the White House from the outside. The story of her rise and ultimate fall is one that will likely go down in history and find its way onto the big screen in some biopic fashion.

Hillary Clinton was called, by many, towards the end of the election, the most qualified candidate ever to seek the office of the president owing to her role as a lawyer, First Lady, Senator, and Secretary of State. She's a highly typical candidate with a resume that seems to match what we're used to seeing. But her campaign was anything but typical.

After all, this is a woman who had been pegged by her fellow students while an undergrad in college that she just might become the first women president. And she very nearly did.

Early Years

Clinton was born in Chicago, Illinois in 1947. In her childhood, she served as a Brownie and Girl Scout as well as an athletic student in both swimming and baseball (Bernstein, 2007). She attended Wellesley College after high school, majoring in political science. While there, she served as president of Wellesley Young Republicans, something that would haunt her later down the road during allegations of "flip-flopping" (Milton, 1999). She noted that, during this time, she found herself in a place of political and internal turmoil, describing herself as someone with a "conservative mind" but "a heart liberal" (Bernstein, 2007). She would eventually, as present events and history would tell us, serve as the democratic Senator for New York and as Secretary of State in a democratic White House.

College Career

Perhaps one of the lesser-known tidbits about Hillary Clinton's years in college, something that was overshadowed during the primary and her debates with Bernie Sanders who was touted as the only candidate to fight during the Civil Rights Movement: after the assignation of Dr. Martin Luther King Jr. she organized a two-day strike and worked with her black fellow students to recruit more black faculty members (Kenney, 1993). Further, in her role as president of Wellesley College Government Association, many of her fellow students remarked that her leadership prevented riots and disruptions on campus, common to other schools at the time, and they believed she might one day become the first woman president (Kenney, 1993).

During her graduation, her fellow students petitions for her to be allowed to serve as a commencement speaker at their graduation, following Senator Brooks, and the result was a standing ovation that lasted 7 minutes (Gerth and Van Natta, 2007). It was during her graduate career at Yale that she met future president, and her future husband, Bill Clinton. He proposed to her, following their graduation in 1973, but she initially declined the proposal and instead went to offer writings and work on the children's right movement, with her article "Children Under the Law" frequently cited by her peers in support of children as competent citizens (Duncan and Sarrl, 1992).

Early Professional Work

After her several years of work in the field of children's rights, she was chosen to serve as an advisor to the House Committee on the Judiciary during the Watergate Scandal. During this time, she served as the legal defense for a man accused of raping a 12-year-old girl, something that has since been cited against her (Contorno, 2014). She called the case "terrible" and, afterward, helped to found the first women's rape crisis center in Fayette (Contorno, 2014).

Despite her continuing doubts about tying her political future and accomplishments to another person, she agreed to marry Bill Clinton in 1975. Clinton continued to work in child and family law over the years and became the First Lady of Arkansas when Bill was elected Governor in 1978. A year later, she became the first woman to become a full partner at Rose Law Firm (Gerth and Van Natta, 2007), in fact, she had a higher salary than her husband until he became president (Bernstein, 2007).

First Lady

During Bill's 1992 campaign for president, she received criticism for her career-first outlook, which was viewed as insulting to those who did engage in stay-at-home life (Burns, 2008), in fact, many drew comparisons between her and Lady Macbeth, especially after Bill referred to his presidency as a "two for one deal" with Hillary taking a prominent role (Toner, 1992). Upon entering into her capacity as First Lady, she was the first among them to have a postgraduate degree and to have a professional career before entering the White House (PBS, 2014).

However, Bill's two-for-one comments came back to haunt that as many viewed the administration as a co-presidency and referred to as the "Billary" administration (Kelly, 1992). In her capacity as First Lady, she focused on health care, specifically on health care for children. However, her status as a power symbol in the White House received a shocking blow in 1998 when investigations revealed the president had an affair with a White House intern, Monica Lewinsky. Bill was impeached by the House but acquitted by the Senate and, despite her public statements of support for her husband, sources claimed she was privately furious with him and considered a divorce

(Bernstein, 2007).

Senator From New York

Despite the struggles faced by the Clintons upon leaving the White House, both in the form of public opinion of legal fees, Hillary was elected to the Senate in the representation of New York in 2000. She served on five Senate committees, including those on a budget, armed services, environment, health and education, and aging. Following the September 11th terrorist attacks, she sought funding for recovery efforts, which amounted to $21 billion. However, one flaw of her time as president that is often cited is her support of the Patriot Act and her support of the military action in Afghanistan (Clinton, 2001). However, she would come to support withdraw of troops from Iraq by 2005 (Fitzgerald, 2005). But 2014, she would call her vote in favor of the war a mistake (Lerner, 2015).

During her time, she also supported the Family Entertainment Protection Act, voted against the Economic Growth and Tax Relief Act of 2001, and opposed the Federal Marriage Amendment that would make same-sex marriage illegal from a constitutional standpoint. She was reelected to a second term in 2006 before announcing in 2007 that she was forming a committee to seek the presidency, something she had been considering since 2003 (Gerth and Van Natta, 2007). She famously lost that campaign in the primary to Barack Obama but would later be appointed his Secretary of State.

Cabinet Member

In her capacity as Secretary of State, she was instrumental in many foreign affairs, including brokering a peace and open border policy between Turkey and Armenia (Landler, 2010), candid discussions with Pakistan students and public figures to repair the United States image (Klein, 2009), and was instrumental in attempts to curtail Iran's nuclear program (Landler, 2010). She was also an outspoken advocate of free Internet. She was also instrumental in the president's reactions to the 2011 Egypt protests (Thrush, 2011). In 2011, she gave a speech to the United Nations in favor of same-sex marriage, calling gay rights human rights and planned to advocate for the protection of gay citizens both at home and internationally.

In 2012, the US Consulate in Benghazi was attacked, killing the US ambassador J. Christopher Stephens as well as three other American citizens. The resulting public opinion on the attacks led Clinton to take responsibility for the security lapses (Labott, 2012). In attacks, Clinton's response, and the subsequent hearings became a point of series controversy for Clinton and were used by her political rivals to damage her reputation and credibility as president.

However, the largest controversy that Clinton faced was that over her use of a private email server, instead of a government issued one, while serving in the Cabinet. After an extensive investigation, it was determined that she never sent or received anything marked classified on her private server (Comey, 2016). Despite the lack of substantial evidence of any wrongdoing, the email controversy and Benghazi hearings damaged Clinton's public image close to her campaign as president. Still, she would as mentioned, win the popular election by almost 3 million votes. But the Electoral College system gave the presidency to Trump.

She would eventually become the fifth candidate in history to win the popular vote but lose the election. And, among those five candidates, the only woman.

CHAPTER 2: THE RISE OF DONALD TRUMP

Hillary Clinton, despite some opposition from Bernie Sanders and his grassroots supporters, was seen as a shoe-in successor to President Obama. And despite winning the election by nearly 3 million votes, she found herself in January of 2017 a private citizen while Donald Trump was sworn in as 45th President of the United States. Many have marked this recent presidential race as one of the total opposites: man vs. woman, feminist vs. macho businessman, left wing beliefs vs. capitalism. It was as much a show of theater as it was a battle of politics. Thanks to the antics of the reality TV show host, much of the race felt more like an episode of television than real, American politics.

But where did this Trump-mania come from? How did a tide of support for Donald Trump come out of nowhere like a tidal wave? Donald Trump is a businessman who made a name for himself, outside of his father's in the 80s and 90s and became a symbol for Manhattan life and real estate business. He'd often talked economics and plans to possibly run for president one day. Those ideas came to fruition in 2016 when he was elected president by the United States.

But never has there been such an unprecedented candidate. Ronald Reagan caught the attention of the world when the actor turned Republican became president of the United States. Today it's a real estate tycoon and reality TV star sitting in the oval office. Where does it begin? And is there evidence in Trump's personal and professional past that prove he's capable of the job he's been assigned or are his detractors right when they say he is unqualified and careening towards a bombastic and early end to his presidency.

Early Years

It begins in 1946 when Donald Trump was born in Queens, New York to Fred Trump, a real-estate developer, and his wife, Scottish immigrant Mary Anne MacLeod. His ancestry through his mother included Scottish while his father was the son of a German immigrant. He attended Kew-Forest School until seventh grade, New York Military Academy at the age of 13 after his parents learned he was taking secret trips into Manhattan, and eventually Fordham University before transferring to Penn's Wharton School of Business where he graduated in 1968 with a Bachelor of Science Degree in Economics. It was during his time at Wharton that he first began venturing into the family business before he graduated.

During his time at school, he was not drafted during the Vietnam War by means of student deferments. He was, at one point given a medical deferment as well for heel spurs, but was eventually assigned a high draft number, making his call to the war highly unlikely.

Real Estate Beginnings

He began his professional career in the family company, Elizabeth Trump and Son, working specifically with middle-class rentals in non-Manhattan boroughs. However, he did have a successful real estate venture, while still in college, in Ohio. In 1971, he became president of the company and his father moved to Chairman of the Board—it was then renamed The Trump Organization. The first possibility of trouble arose during this time when, in 1973, his father became the subject of the Justice Department when he was accused of discriminating against African Americans in their rental business (Dunlap, 2015). In 1978, Trump moved into Manhattan, purchasing and remodeling his first commercial property in the form of a Hyatt. It was also in this year that he negotiated the development of Trump Tower, completed in 1983. Today Trump Tower includes a full film studio where *The Apprentice* is filmed. He continued real estate ventures throughout the decades, revitalizing hotels in New York, purchasing properties in Palm Beach and Atlantic City, as well as golf courses in Scotland.

Trump can be credited with taking his father's real estate ventures and turning them into a massive, multibillion-dollar industry by branching out of Manhattan and out of rental properties alone. Trump's purchase of the Commodore Hotel in 1978 was the first foray of the company into the commercial business real estate. Trump and his father turned it into a Grand Hyatt Hotel, located in the prime location right next to Grand Central Station. Trump also finished a remodeling project in Central part that was past its 2 ½ year completion schedule, finishing it in 3 months, under budget.

What can be said for Trump's business beginners is this: he turned a company into a corporation. He turned a business of apartment rentals into a total luxury living empire. He aimed big and hit the mark several times during his early tenure as the head of his family's company. But are his business chops enough to say he's qualified to be president?

He first talked seriously about running for office on a platform to save the economy when the Great Recession took place. Since then, the platform has obviously changed with his focus on immigration and preventing terrorism at home, something, objectively, he has much less experience at while looking at his resume of work thus far.

Family Life

Trump, in total, has been married three times and has 5 children and 8 grandchildren as a result. His first wife was Ivana Zelnickova, originally from Czechoslovakia before it was dismantled into the Czech Republic and Slovakia. They married in 1977 and had Trump's three eldest children: Donald Jr., Ivanka, and Eric. All three of his children would eventually be given places in the family business. The couple had a highly publicized divorce in 1992.

Trump's second wife was Marla Maples, whom he had started seeing before his relationship with Ivana ended. They had one child, Tiffany, during their marriage which lasted from 1993 to 1999. His third and final wife—and future First Lady--Melania Knauss is a Slovene Model and the couple has one son, Barron.

Currently, Eric and Donald both have taken over management of the Trump real estate business while their father is in office and Ivanka, who was the Executive Vice President of the Trump Organization, resigned from the company to work as an official assistant to her father as president. The move, seen by many as dangerous nepotism, has been criticized as a possible breach in security and a conflict of interests.

It has been postulated that Ivanka Trump was responsible for Trump's leniency on Planned Parenthood, which he promised to defund only to back off of and offer a deal. Whether this influence should be seen as good or bad, remains to be seen.

Legal Issues

However, things weren't always as well kept as Trump as often reported, as of 2016, his company had been the subject of over 3,500 legal cases at the state and federal level. Of that, 1,900 featured Trump as the plaintiff, mainly dealing with gamblers who did not pay off debts, but 1,400 featured Trump as the defendant (Savransky, 2016). His casinos and hotels have declared bankruptcy six times, incidents that Trump referred to as him "playing with bankruptcy laws" in order to keep his businesses open while they went through negotiations (Stone, 2011).

As of today, Trump has not been officially named as one of those under investigation by the FBI for Russian influence in the presidential election. Though, it has been released that Trump did question Comey as to whether he was under investigation himself. As far as we know, the focus had been Flynn. So, Trump's situation with the FBI currently has not been proven as an investigation.

Jack of Many Trades

In the course of his career, he's worked with in professional sports, beauty pageants, charitable organizations, and the controversial Trump University. The Trump Foundation has not received personal donations from Trump in almost 10 years (Fahrenhold and Heldeman, 2016). Trump University is now defunct following lawsuits from the State of New York for defraudment, false statements, and illegal use of the word "university" (Halperin, 2016). Trump also was the host of the reality television show *The Apprentice*.

It was first in 1987 that Trump publically talked about the idea of running for president. He seriously considered it in 1988, 2000, 2004, and 2012. In all cases, Trump stated he would run as a Republican. He officially entered the race in 2015 and eventually went on to win the Republican nomination and, eventually, the Electoral vote. But how does a businessman whose abilities were described by *The Economist* as "mediocre" in 2016 (Economist, 2016) become president of the United States?

Sordid Personality

There's a lot of complicated facets involved with Trump's popularity and Hillary's decline. Despite the victories, Trump's road to the presidency was not without major hiccups and reputation hurting incidents dug up from his past. The same, of course, can be said for Hillary.

It's difficult to trace Donald Trump's history with the same effectiveness as Hillary's because most of what he's done has been view retroactively: deals he's made, properties he's bought, all have no caught the attention of the world until he stepped out onto the debate stage. But some things should not be shoved under the rug, and that goes for both Clinton and Trump.

So perhaps the best method is less a factual recall of their professional histories and more an in-depth look at where they stand on certain policies, what they've said about certain policies, and choices they've made as a result.

Much of the scandals involving Trump and his controversial views will be touched upon in a later chapter in this book.

CHAPTER 3: EMAILS, EMAILS, EMAILS

Easily one of the most repeated phrases during this election was "Hillary's emails." The GOP often cited her use of a personal Gmail server for government information as a reason to deem her untrustworthy and irresponsible as a candidate. And much of the public agreed that it wasn't a smart move and even dangerous for the safety of national security and vital information. A lot of buzzwords were thrown around regarding the emails and Trump very vocally threatened to incarcerate Clinton when he became president as a result of her carelessness.

But what's the truth here? What does the phrase "Hillary's emails" actually mean? And what was the reason behind using a private Gmail server while acting as Secretary of State?

Origin of the Frenzy

In March 2015, it was made public that Hillary Clinton had utilized a Gmail server, while Secretary of State, to send and receive emails to fellow government officials and aids. The root of this decision can be traced to Clinton's steadfast use of BlackBerry devices that she and all her official aids communicated on. The information on this BlackBerry was stored in a private server in her home in Upstate New York. The domains she set up, hosted on the server, were clintonemail.com, wjcoffice.com and presidentclinton.com. She utilized data systems and a firm to manage the email system.

In 2009, the National Archives and Records Administration first expressed concerns about Clinton going out of the normal government regulated data and record keeping system. Things took a turn in 2013 when a hacker was able to break into the clintonemail.com server and distribute some emails found there, specifically ones dealing with the 2012 Benghazi attack. At the time the emails were non-classified but have been retroactively done so by the State Department. In 2014, the State Department began an investigation on 12 boxes full of emails, though some 31,000 had been deleted and unrecovered as of May 2016.

So, what are the issues here? The first is the use of a private email server, independently monitored, to send and receive official emails. Though none had been marked classified at the time of their sending, the 2013 hack proved to be detrimental to both Clinton's image and national security when Benghazi information was leaked. The other issue, one that many focused on, was the possibility that Clinton was trying to hide something by using the private email server. But was that the case?

The fact of the matter is, Clinton was incredibly transparent during her investigation compared to a Republican analogue, George W. Bush, whose administration "lost" 22 million emails written between 2003 and 2009 (Newsweek, 2016). It also turns out that the Bush administration utilized a non-government, private email server as well but failed to store them and, on top of that, refused a subpoena from congress requesting access to the emails (Newweek, 2016). The reason for this private server use was the frequent blackouts in the White House email system.

Do you remember hearing about the Bush email scandal? Probably not.

George Bush's Little Known Email Scandal

The fact of the matter is, the first iteration of what would become a White House Email system was set up during the Reagan administration and in 1981, Congress passed the PRA (Presidential Records Act) that mandated records of the Executive branch be preserved that they belonged to the collective public of the United States. However, that mandate didn't exactly convince the Bush information from actually doing it. The Clinton Administration set up an automated email archive that generated a warning dialogue box if someone attempted to delete any emails, which, evidently, Bush ignored (Newsweek, 2016). Bush's emails came into question after the firing of nine U.S. attorneys that was believed the politically motivated, however, emails incriminating those actions were lost (Newsweek, 2016).

So, in comparison, was Hillary Clinton's email situation really all that much worse? Granted, the use of private servers by anyone seems irresponsible considering the outlines of the PRA. However, Clinton was not the president nor vice president at the time (the two members of the Executive branch to whom that mandate applied). Hacking seems to be an inevitable part of the digital world and danger to any server. Whether or not you want to blame politicians for their control of their own emails are up to you. But these are the facts of the email situation and, as of mid-2017, no charges have been brought against Hillary Clinton for criminal activity.

I NEED YOUR HELP

I really want to thank you again for reading this book. Hopefully you have liked it so far and have been receiving value from it. Lots of effort was put into making sure that it provides as much content as possible to you and that I cover as much as I can.

If you've found this book helpful, then I'd like to ask you a favor. Would you be kind enough to leave a review for it on Amazon? It would be greatly appreciated!

CHAPTER 4: HACKS FROM ALL SIDES

If there was one word that defined 2016 it was probably hacked. Whether it be someone discussing the hacks on Hillary Clinton's email server or someone talking about the hack on the DNC. This was a presidential race waged on a digital battleground. Though, looking at the facts, the situation with the hacking and who was targeted was incredibly one-sided, which has led many to suspect that the Russians, who supported Trump's presidency, attempted to sabotage the Democratic party by *Game of Thrones* level tactics and carefully released streams of emails.

If nothing else, this is an incredibly fascinating digital age of elections. Never before has digital warfare been so present, whether factually or mentioned, in a presidential race. Recently, the term "cyber warfare" was officially named in 2010 as a form of warfare alongside naval, air, and land. It is considered a terrain in combat and this may be the first time it's been utilized to its fullest extent in any conflict or shadow conflict. This, again, makes the situation an interesting one, if not a scary one. Depending on what is uncovered by the FBI and CIA, this could be the dawning of an age where digital battles are waged between countries, which would be a much harder tactic to fight.

The Origins of Discontent

The issue of hacks goes back to a place that you might not suspect: Hillary Clinton's primaries challenger, Bernie Sanders. Third party candidates have always been something of a thorn for the members of the two big parties. They split the vote and, more often than not, that vote splitting is more detrimental on the democrats as there are more left-leaning third parties than right.

Bernie Sanders, the junior Senator from Vermont, announced in April 2015 that he intended to seek the Democratic party's nomination for president. He is a registered Independent and the longest serving Independent in Congress. Sanders' campaign caught the attention and the hearts of idealistic young liberals across the country with his lack of Super PAC funding, refusal of money from wealthy donors. His campaign promises included raising the minimum wage, free health care, legalization of marijuana, among other far left ideals.

He quickly became an overnight sensation as a candidate. Despite running as a democrat, he was technically a registered third party politician which gave independents their first real shot at getting a none major party candidate into the White House, though some did get jumpy at Sanders' self-identification as a democratic socialist. It was an exciting time, but not everyone in the Democratic Party was excited. As it would be revealed in email leaks, the DNC was profusely against Sanders getting the nomination and stalwart in promoting Clinton for the nomination. This idea of predetermining the presidential candidates angered a great many of Sanders supporters and furthered the idea that Clinton and the DNC were elitist and out of touch with the common people.

Things got heated when followers of the Sanders campaign claimed they were being treated unfairly by the media and not given adequate time, with most outlets operating under the assumption that Hillary was the automatic nominee. There was also calls of favoritism on the part of the DNC that lead to a massive hacking scandal that portrayed their treatment of Sanders in a highly negative light.

The emails were so vitriolic towards Sanders and his supporters that the DNC issued an official apology to the group for the language used and the apparent plotting to deny Sanders the nomination. Despite that, and despite Sanders accepting the apology, the emails did their work in dividing the party, ostracizing Bernie Sanders' supporters from the larger fold of the DNC and hurting the chances of converting his voters to Clinton instead of a third party candidate.

Though, when Sanders eventually lost the nomination, he did urge his followers to throw their passion into keeping Trump out of the White House by supporting Hillary, bad blood lingered in great amounts among the Sanders' supporters and traditional Democratic supporters. Though it cannot be quantified at this point, that discontent may have been a factor in Clinton's loss to Trump.

Seeing Red

In December 2016, the CIA formally accused Russia was responsible for the hack in an effort to undermine Hillary Clinton's campaign (Time, 2016). Though Russia and Trump both outright denied their responsibility in the situation. Specifically, the CIA accused the higher up positions in the Kremlin of having direct ties to the WikiLeaks hackers and accepting information from them to disperse to the public (Time, 2016). Despite the widespread conclusion of the Russia hackers and the CIA's reveal that the hackers were previously known entities to them, Donald Trump denied the claims that Russia was in any way trying to help him win the election.

The leaks divided the democratic party in the hopes of getting voters away from Hillary Clinton. Whether or not it worked is something up for endless debate. But it wasn't the end of the hacking scandal in the election. In fact, several months after the inauguration, we're still discussing it and what it means for the future of the country.

The emails scandals weren't done. Clinton, in the wake of her loss, condemned Russia for the "weaponizing of information" (New York Times, 2017). She even went as far to claim that the hacks weren't the end of it, that a fairly well organized online assault that included bots spread false information to discredit her. She also warned that thanks to the success of their efforts, they won't easily go away and might continue to meddle in US affairs in a similar fashion now that they know it can be done.

Clickbait Warfare

The email hacks, no matter where they came from, did do their job. They revealed DNC infighting and infighting in the Clinton campaign as well. While not entirely unheard of, to see it splayed out for all to see was highly damaging for the Clinton campaign and it also effectively blended two separate topics in the minds of voters: DNC hacks and Clinton's email server. It worked in glorious favor with buzzword click bait and the age of "fake news." It further pushed some of the darker parts of Clinton and her campaign, however.

One of the biggest complaints about Clinton, her campaign, and the DNC as a whole, was the lack of understanding of the common voter. The word most often thrown around on this front was "out of touch." And the emails leaked didn't help that image when Robby Mook, Clinton's eventual campaign manager, used the phrase "The Clintons won't forget what their friends have done for them" (BBC, 2016). This was only furthered by calls for the Clinton's to release the contents of their paid speeches and demands for answers from the DNC for its treatment of Bernie Sanders.

Airing of Faults

There were some policy issues revealed as well. According to one email, Clinton wanted to covertly intervene in Syria (BBC, 2016). This email did not help her image as a "war hawk" in the eyes of more left leaning liberals (Bernie Sanders among them). She also warned China that they would be forced to install missile defense systems near North Korea if China could not control them (BBC, 2016). There was also attacks against Catholic Conservatives by her communications director Jennifer Palmieri and Clinton's own belief that politics should be like a "like a sausage being made" where the end product is acceptable so long as the consumers don't know how they got there (BBC, 2016).

There were plenty of other blips that happened in the form of trade deals, refugee policy, debate questions, and other interpersonal drama. It all added up to a stewing pot, ready to boil over and ruin the reputation of the Clinton campaign in the last few weeks of the election.

The Kremlin continues to deny it and Donald Trump also denies that he is in the pocket of Russia or owes a debt to them at all. But, that hasn't convinced many Americans. Further, it hasn't convinced the FBI who opened an investigation on the matter that has led to one of the most unprecedented moments of presidential abuse of power in history.

CHAPTER 5: TRUMP AND RUSSIA: A LOVE STORY

When the Trump campaign began, many people considered it a fluke, a passing fade, something that would disappear after the first couple of debates. But then the leaks happened, the hacks, and all sorts of nonsense over on the DNC side of things that lead many to suspect someone was deliberately trying to sabotage the Clinton campaign through digital warfare. Fingers quickly pointed towards WikiLeaks and Julian Assange, which quickly turned to Russia.

A Brief History of America and Russia

Never in life have there been two countries that have more personified the story of a tragic fall from grace from friends to bitter enemies. The two superpowers of the world emerged victorious post-World War II and immediately set their sights on each other as enemies. Russia, a place of political turmoil since the overthrow of the tsar had settled on a form of absolute communism and pseudo-Marxism that flew in the face of American ideals of capitalism and democracy.

After the two countries punched their way into Nazi Germany from either side and took scientists captive, it became an arms race like no other when the Manhattan Project took full effect and the United States ended the war in Japan with a devastating blow of two atomic bombs. What followed as a period commonly known as the Cold War, a time of tension that saw several proxy wars (Vietnam and Korea) between not necessarily Russia and the United States directly, but between government ideals and the monopoly on world peace the United States was trying to put in place (pax Americana).

When the Berlin Wall fell in the late 20th century, tensions did not go away and current president Vladimir Putin has been accused of continuing the USSR traditions in non-official ways (such as his forced "election" to another term as president and laws against criticizing him). This has never sat well with the Executive branch of the United States. And with the new election, the possibility that Russia has somehow affected the outcome has shaken the American people.

The United States has never had a truly easy relationship with Russia and it was made even worse by the possibility that they have now not only rigged their own elections, as many claim them have but attempted to do the same with the United States. However, this isn't simply a witch hunt and crying wolf. Russia role was calculated and precise and it starts with political criminal Julian Assange, hiding out, currently in the Ecuadorian embassy in London.

Assange's Role

Julian Assange, a trained programmer, is a hacker who founded WikiLeaks 2006, a website devoted to posting information obtained from leaks and hacking of classified information. It did not gain international attention until it began posting information on Chelsea Manning, specifically on the United States' activities in the Middle East and evidence of prisoner treatment in Guantanamo Bay.

After the continued trials of Chelsea Manning and the investigation on Assange, he looked for political asylum while continuing to do work for WikiLeaks, responsible for the many hacked emails and information on Hillary Clinton and the DNC.

In February 2016, Assange released a criticism of Clinton, though WikiLeaks' official stance was that it was not picking and choosing which candidate's information to release (Bloomberg, 2016). The connection to Russia comes in when the CIA confirmed it was highly certain that Vladimir Putin had personally ordered hackers to perform an "influence campaign" against Hillary and send information gathered to WikiLeaks (New York Times, 2017). Things were further made murky when Trump was asked during a debate if he would condemn Russian leaks and in his response, promising to condemn "anyone" who hacks the US, he left out Putin (Mail Online, 2016). Trump has since been called by many "Putin's puppet" for his passive role in apparently accepting help from the Russians to win his campaign and allowing them to further integrate themselves into foreign affairs.

The connection between WikiLeaks and Russia has yet to be proven—or if it has, that information has not been released to the general public. The accusation is that WikiLeaks is responsible for the hack and offering the information to Russia has been denied by WikiLeaks and Putin's apparent call for hackers to take action in the election has also not been established in connection with WikiLeaks. That being said, many believe circumstantial evidence proves Assange and WikiLeaks' involvement and contact with Russia in the process.

The FBI Steps In

Shortly into Trump's presidency, FBI Director Comey, someone that Trump previously lauded for his investigation of Clinton, announced the FBI was investigating his administration, campaign, and himself for ties to Russia and any involvement in hacking and leaks from Russia and WikiLeaks. What made, even more, news was when Trump, shortly after this was made public, fired the FBI Director. It turns out, Trump asked Comey several times if he was under investigation and, shortly before the termination, warned him to end his investigation of Trump advisor Michael Flynn. The move shook many, as it was seen as an obstruction of justice and an impeachable offense. Not to mention, it did nothing to discredit the theory that Trump was someone aided by Russia in his election.

As it turns out, Michael Flynn had at least 18 undisclosed communications with Kremlin officials since spring 2016 (Reuters, 2017). Disturbingly, some of the communications close to the election were on the topic of setting up a "backchannel" communication line for Trump and Putin to bypass the US national security regulations (Reuters, 2017). Comey first met with Trump on February 14th, 2017 where Trump, reportedly, told him to halt his investigation of Flynn, who had since been relieved of his official duties (LA Times, 2017). On March 20th the investigation was made public after a month of Trump tweeting denials of his connection to

Russia (LA Times, 2017). Later that month, Flynn asked for an immunity deal in exchange for full cooperation in testifying in Congress on the investigation and, the next month, Carter Page, Trump's campaign advisor, was named as a possible Russian agent who had been monitored by the FBI since summer 2016 (LA Times, 2017). Testifying and calls between Trump and Putin continue until May 9th when Trump fires Comey, citing his mishandling of the Clinton email investigation as the cause (LA Times, 2017). The next day, Trump met with Russian Foreign Minister Sergey Lavrov and Ambassador Sergey Kislyak and, on the 15th of May, the Washington Post reported that Trump had shared classified information on ISIS with Russia (LA Times, 2017).
It's not a pretty picture.

What is clear, whether Trump was party to it or not, there was interference from an outside party, that was likely Russia, to get Trump into the White House. What does that mean for his presidency? Well it's another part of it that's completely unprecedented in the course of American history but, depending on how Trump reacts, it could become grounds for the undermining of the entire administration if he is impeached as a result of meddling with justice or knowingly accepting foreign aid in the form of digital attacks on US citizens.

The one fact is that the facts don't stop. Each day something new comes out, whether it helps or hurts Trump's chances at improving his image, they continue to flood the news waves and the desks of government officials.

Is It True?

One of the biggest things that seem to be stopping everyone from acting on the situation is the lack of assurance that it's actually happening. As Clinton once said, politics are like a sausage, something we don't get to see the creation of, just the result. This idea is reaffirmed in the highly popular Broadway show about Alexandra Hamilton and the birth of the nation, *Hamilton*, where Aaron Burr, desperate for a seat of power, compares politics to make a sausage and that no one is truly in "the room where it happens."

The fact is, the CIA can postulate and the American public can share their opinions but no one really knows what's going on or how it happened. The facts are outlined above: Trump's advisors had contact with Russia before the election, we don't know if Trump himself was party to these communications before he became president, we know Trump has shared classified information on ISIS with Russian officials and barred certain news outlets from the White House while allowing Russia outlets in.

If this were a courtroom, we'd be looking at a mass of circumstantial evidence but no smoking gun. There are no fingerprints or witnesses. There's a lot of contexts that makes it seem like it happened but no real proof. And without proof, no one can do anything about it. There are only the continuing accusations and the lack of justice for any party. This is also the first serious talk of impeachment since Bill Clinton, possibly worse than that to be compared only to Nixon's wire taping.

But, again, that's only if something can be proven. Right now it's investigations and things that people are sharing between each other and what they think they know about the situation.

CHAPTER 6: COMPARING SCANDALS

Both Trump and Clinton were incredibly high profile candidates, possibly the highest-profile candidates in history. Donald Trump, a real estate tycoon, reality TV show host, and a beauty pageant promoter against Hillary Clinton, the former first lady to a painful legacy of impeachment and sexual scandals inside the White House, often criticized as power seeking. They were also both the two most unpopular candidates to ever seek the office of the president, with many comparing the election to a "lesser of two evils" choice.

But how do those scandals stack up against each other? Are they equally guilty of some gossip causing schemes and possibly even crimes?

Scandals themselves are such an interesting concept. It's the public airing of dirty laundry where a high profile person is concerned. Sometimes it's as simple as a faux pa, saying something a little too blunt, or having a tantrum that got caught on camera. Sometimes it's must more serious; sexual assault, arrests, public fights, and the like. Where Clinton and Trump are concerned, their scandals vary in degrees and in topic. Trump's scandals (before the issues of Russian influence) seemed relegated to the world of celebrity and reality television (with some legal blips). Hillary's scandals involved national security and government bodies.

The Many Mistakes of Donald Trump

You could trace Trump's first scandal all the way back to his childhood when he would frequently go to Manhattan without permission which landed him in the military academy as punishment. That bout of rebellious youth, however, was nothing compared to the things that would eventually become of Donald Trump and his public image. During the course of his run for office, he was the center of no less than 25 scandals. Picking through them results in some unfortunate consistencies: view on women, tax evasion, and loose cannon statements.

One of the first and biggest scandals for Trump was his tiff with Fox reporter and debate moderator Megyn Kelly. During the debate, Kelly pressed Trump on his comments on women and he fired right back. But things got worse when Trump commented on her saying "Blood coming out of her eyes, blood coming out of her wherever" (ABC News 2016). As a result of the feud, Megyn Kelly was let go from Fox News and Trump did nothing to help shake his image as a sexist or even a misogynist.

On that front, things only got worse when a tape of Trump in 2005 was released that heard Trump talking about women in his pageants and how he attempted to seduce several women in the pageant using very blunt language, the most cited of which was "Grab them by the pussy" when discussing actress Arianne Zucker (Slate, 2016). Trump defended it as locker room banter that was leaked to the public.

Aside from his insults to women, Trump has insulted other groups as well, in this case, war veterans and prisoners of war, specifically, Senator John McCain. During the campaign, Trump remarked that the Senator from Arizona was only a hero because he was captured and that he "liked people who weren't captured" (The Guardian, 2015). A little history on this situation: while Trump received several student deferments from the Vietnam draft while he was in college, Senator McCain was held prisoner by forces in North Vietnam for over five years and tortured to the point where he is unable to lift his arms because they had been broken and the bones reset so many times. He went on to call McCain a "dummy" for graduating last in his Naval Academy class (The Guardian, 2016).

Trump insulted Mexican citizens and Mexican immigrants to America on a number of occasions as well. He suggested that second amendment activists could do something about it if Hillary Clinton became president, he insulted the Jewish populations with an anti-Hillary ad featuring a Star of David. As mentioned, there are almost thirty in the span of one year. And as previously outlined, Trump also faced some severe uphill legal battles where his properties and handling of his companies was concerned.

How Do Clinton's Failures Compare?

But what about Hillary? Where do her scandals rank in the grand scheme of this campaign? As we know, the biggest scandal associated with her at this point is her emails and the use of a private email server for government business. We also know her in ties to the Clinton sex scandal in the 90s when her husband was president. She will forever be tied to the DNC email hack as well as she was often the subject of their back and forth emails to each other.

So how do these scandals compare? Trump often found himself in hot water with the media over things he said that were insulting to certain groups, both presently and retroactively. Clinton found herself caught in a political windstorm. But is that worse? After all, Clinton's credibility was often at stake in the election, as was her leadership skills. Even if her scandals weren't of a childish variety, dealing with gossip and poor judgment in interviews, it was her own decision making a record that was in question: the emails, her stance on the war in Iraq, her beliefs on US presence in the Middle East. These things helped shaped an idea of her and were far louder to most voters than her work as a lawyer and champion of children and women, as scandals often go.

But does that mean the election really was the lesser of two evils? Were the American people truly forced to choice between two equally unqualified candidates or was something else at work in the minds of the American public that goes deeper than politics and deeper than records? There's a lot of variables in this election and the fact that a woman was seeking the presidency in the most legitimate female driven campaign yet can't go unnoticed.

What Do Scandals Mean?

Every president and every presidential candidate have scandals. Philosophically this is the nature of being human, faults and mistakes. But the interesting things about scandals is how we rank them and how they compare. It seems every election is the comparison of past mistakes and whoever made the least gets to be president—or whoever had enough triumphs to outweigh them. Whether or not he was considered mediocre by certain outlets, he's an accomplished businessman and his skills as a negotiator have been praised by many of his business partners and rivals. He also was one of many who helped revitalize tourism in Manhattan in the 1980s when the image of the city and the safety of tourists was at an all-time low.

But he's been subject to thousands of lawsuits (many are run by the mill suits of disgruntled visitors) and has been on the record several times as a perceived enemy of women's rights. His company has a history of racial discrimination going back to his father and Trump single greatest enemy in this campaign has been Mexican immigrants to American whom he ostracized with promises to build a wall at the border and deport thousands.

One could also view his situation with the Russians as simply a way to restore ties with the country, while some view it as intrigue and espionage and lies from the highest office. It depends on your perception and what you want to see before facts finally hit the light.

As for Hillary Clinton, her scandals are almost exclusive to the political arena, choices she made in the past that many find to be poor. She supported the war in Iraq but didn't always support gay rights. She was once a republican and helped defend a man accused of raping a young girl (a case she has often condemned and deeply regretted). But while in college her leadership skills shined to her fellow students who requested her as their commencement speaker and believed she would one day be president. She worked tirelessly as a full partner lawyer and made children and families her priorities during her tenure as First Lady and during her time as a Senator.

But she also has changed her political stance on things many times. She's been accused of being "out of touch" as a political elitist and one of the most sought after political allies in Washington today. She's been called irresponsible for her email choices and the situation in Benghazi.

So where does it all stand? Scandals in politics are not like those that appear in Star magazine or other tabloids. They shake the country and they come from those who shape the nation, which is something the world does not forget easy. What is clear is there have never been two more scandalous candidates running against each other.

CONCLUSION

So what is there to take away from this? Is there anything we're truly able to take from this or was it all a dark time in the history of America? The fact of the matter is, never has the country been more divided since the Civil War and, unlike that time, the lines here weren't clear. It wasn't just democrat vs. republican and north vs. south. Democrats were fighting amongst each other, republicans were doing the same, and all the while those that truly did support either candidate were very busy yelling at each other about the entire situation.

And where do we stand now? We won't know what could have become of a Clinton administration. We'll never know. Mrs. Clinton has now thrown her efforts into the Onward Together project aimed at getting kids, especially minority groups, into politics and running for office. Effectively, she's handing off the torch to the next generation. Her bid for president and the chances of her becoming America's first female president are gone now. What's left is a republican administration that has been accused of fascism, xenophobia, ties to Russia, and obstruction of justice, among other claims.

Opinions have been blurred into fact where many people are concerned in this presidential race and the current administration. The term "fake news" has not only become commonplace among people, but it's also a real problem. Facebook has implemented ways to help fight the fake news on their site and college courses are even being offered for the study and detection of fake news to help prevent clickbait, untruthful articles from getting to the mass public.

On that front, this book has striven to be as factual as possible, searching out sources and checking them for validity. So many things during the election were so highly publicized that it almost seems like common knowledge itself can be the source of information. But in this age, this book has strived to give you real, factual information with sources both in the form of what you know and what the news has to say.

The election results, however they happened, are final and in. Donald Trump is president, though many deny this legitimacy and have called for investigations and impeachment. Every day the news updates and the context of the world we're in changes. New information appears old information becomes obsolete. It's a difficult climate to keep up with. We live in an extremely interesting time in American history if nothing else.

SOURCES

The following sources are listed in the order they appear in the text above to avoid accusations of false information.

http://www.cnn.com/2016/12/21/politics/donald-trump-hillary-clinton-popular-vote-final-count/

http://www.latimes.com/politics/washington/la-na-essential-washington-updates-comey-emails-1494374889-htmlstory.html

https://www.theguardian.com/us-news/2017/feb/24/media-blocked-white-house-briefing-sean-spicer

http://www.nbcnews.com/politics/white-house/what-you-need-know-about-trump-comey-russia-probe-n757191

https://www.nytimes.com/2017/05/10/us/politics/trump-russia-meeting-american-reporters-blocked.html

Bernstein, Carl (2007). *A Woman in Charge: The Life of Hillary Rodham Clinton*. New York: Alfred A. Knopf.ISBN 0-375-40766-9.
*Milton, Joyce (1999). The First Partner: Hillary Rodham Clinton. William Morrow and Company. ISBN 0-688-15501-4.*pp. 27–28
*Milton, Joyce (1999). The First Partner: Hillary Rodham Clinton. William Morrow and Company. ISBN 0-688-15501-4.*pp. 27–28

Gerth, Jeff; Van Natta, Don Jr. (2007). *Her Way: The Hopes and Ambitions of Hillary Rodham Clinton*. New York: Little, Brown and Company. ISBN 0-316-01742-6.
Gerth, Jeff; Van Natta, Don Jr. (2007). *Her Way: The Hopes and Ambitions of Hillary Rodham Clinton*. New York: Little, Brown and Company. ISBN 0-316-01742-6.
Contorno, Steve (July 17, 2014)."Did Hillary Clinton ask to be 'relieved' from representing an accused rapist in 1970s?". PolitiFact.

Defeat Amnesia: Hillary Clinton Comments in 2008
Toner, Robin (September 24, 1992)."Backlash for Hillary Clinton Puts

Negative Image to Rout". _The New York Times._

Hillary Rodham Clinton". _PBS._ _Retrieved December 2, 2014._ Clinton had the first postgraduate degree through regular study and scholarly work. Eleanor Roosevelt had been previously awarded a postgraduate honorary degree. Clinton's successor Laura Bushbecame the second first lady with a postgraduate degree

Kelly, Michael (January 20, 1993)."The First Couple: A Union of Mind and Ambition"_. The New York Times._

Clinton, Hillary (November 24, 2001)."New Hope For Afghanistan's Women". _Time._

Fitzgerald, Jim (November 21, 2005)."Hillary Clinton says immediate withdrawal from Iraq would be 'a big mistake'"_. U-T San Diego. Associated Press._

Lerner, Adam (May 19, 2015). "Hillary Clinton says her Iraq war vote was a 'mistake'"_. Politico._

Landler, Mark (September 4, 2010). "In Middle East Peace Talks, Clinton Faces a Crucial Test". _The New York Times._

lein, Joe (November 5, 2009)."The State of Hillary: A Mixed Record on the Job". _Time._

Richter, Paul; Pierson, David (January 23, 2010). "Sino-U.S. ties hit new snag over Internet issues". _Los Angeles Times._

Thrush, Glenn (February 2, 2011)."Hillary Clinton plays key role in dance with Hosni Mubarak". _Politico._

Labott, Elise (October 16, 2012)."Clinton: I'm responsible for diplomats' security". CNN.

Statement by FBI Director James B. Comey on the Investigation of Secretary Hillary Clinton's Use of a Personal E-Mail System". Fbi.gov. July 5, 2016. Archived from the original on July 17, 2016. Retrieved July 12, 2016.

Kelly, Conor (July 27, 2015). "Meet Donald Trump: Everything You Need To Know (And Probably Didn't Know) About The 2016 Republican Presidential Candidate". ABC News.

Dunlap, David (July 30, 2015). "1973: Meet Donald Trump". _The New York Times._Archived

Savransky, Rebecca (June 2, 2016). "Trump brags about winning record in lawsuits"

Stone, Peter (May 5, 2011). "Donald Trump's lawsuits could turn off conservatives who embrace tort reform"_. The Center for Public Integrity._

Retrieved March 14, 2016.

Fahrenthold, David A.; Helderman, Rosalind S. (April 10, 2016). "Missing from Trump's list of charitable giving: His own personal cash". *The Washington Post.*

Halperin, David (March 3, 2016). "NY Court Refuses to Dismiss Trump University Case, Describes Fraud Allegations". *The Huffington Post.*
"From the Tower to the White House". *The Economist.* February 20, 2016. RetrievedFebruary 29, 2016. Mr Trump's performance has been mediocre compared with the stockmarket and property in New York.
Broomfield, Matt. "Women's March against Donald Trump is the largest day of protests in US history, say political scientists".*Independent.* Retrieved January 25, 2017.
http://www.ontheissues.org/celeb/Donald_Trump_Abortion.htm
https://www.theguardian.com/commentisfree/2017/jan/24/trump-once-said-women-should-be-punished-for-abortion-t
https://www.nytimes.com/2017/03/10/opinion/trumps-abortion-strategy.html
http://time.com/4422723/putin-russia-hillary-clinton/
https://www.nytimes.com/2017/04/06/nyregion/hillary-clinton-russia-hacking-election-trump.html
http://www.bbc.com/news/world-us-canada-37639370
"How Julian Assange Turned WikiLeaks Into Trump's Best Friend".*Bloomberg.com.* Retrieved 27 October2016.
Intelligence Report on Russian Hacking". The New York Times. January 6, 2017. p. 11. RetrievedJanuary 8, 2017
"Trump and Clinton clash on Putin as she says he's Kremlin's puppet". *Mail Online.* Retrieved 21 October 2016.
http://www.reuters.com/article/us-usa-trump-russia-contacts-idUSKCN18E106
http://www.latimes.com/politics/la-na-pol-trump-flynn-comey-russia-timeline-2017-htmlstory.html
http://abcnews.go.com/Politics/history-donald-trump-megyn-kelly-feud/story?id=36526503
http://www.slate.com/blogs/the_slatest/2016/10/07/donald_tr

ump_2005_tape_i_grab_women_by_the_pussy.html
https://www.theguardian.com/us-news/2015/jul/18/donald-trump-john-mccain-vietnam-iowa-republicans

LIKE THIS BOOK?

Check us out online or follow us on social media for exclusive deals and news on new releases!

 https://www.pinnaclepublish.com

 https://www.facebook.com/PinnaclePublishers/

 https://twitter.com/PinnaclePub

 https://www.instagram.com/pinnaclepublishers/

www.ingramcontent.com/pod-product-compliance
Lightning Source LLC
Chambersburg PA
CBHW061804280526
45787CB00003BA/1475